Baltimore Album Legacy

by Elly Sienkiewicz

❧

Catalog of C&T Publishing's
Baltimore Album Revival Quilt Show
and Contest

❧

Pacific International Quilt Show
Santa Clara, CA
October 8-11, 1998

C&T PUBLISHING

When, at the turn of the 21st century, we take stock of who we are and where we're going, the columns remembered and pediments recollected mark our most contemporary architecture. The style taps the root of Western civilization, paying our cultural wellsprings homage as we embrace the future. Quiltmaking, too, revives the classic, stitching the fiber of our heritage into the fabric of the unknown. In Baltimore-style Album Quilts, the application of cloth to cloth has always been a ritual expression, as transforming to the maker as to the object made. This historic exhibition honors the old made new. It pays tribute to the Revivalist Baltimores, to their makers, and to *Baltimore Beauties and Beyond, Studies in Classic Album Quilt Appliqué,* the ten-book series by Elly Sienkiewicz.

Great numbers of modern quiltmakers have mastered the intricacies of this classic mid-19th century art needlework and caused the style's full-scale revival. Album Quilts reborn are again a brilliantly expressive medium. With this Second Baltimore Revival Exhibition, C&T Publishing celebrates these quilts as history in-the-making and applauds their creators.

This Exhibit Catalog includes:

- Biographical Sketches of the Judges and the Judging Philosophy
- Contest Categories
- Honored Teacher Award Nominees
- Author's Preface
- Journal Excerpt on Judging: "These Are the Quilts That Make You Cry"
- Author's Underlinings and Marginalia (literary quotes to express Album-making's magic)
- Color Portraits of 32 Album Quilts on Exhibition
- Roll Call of Quilts and their makers juried in and hung in the exhibition
- About the Author

Acknowledgments

Baltimore Legacy quiltmakers, you make C&T Publishing's second Baltimore Album Revival Quilt Show and Contest possible —Thank you, once again! To C&T Publishing's fine team, captained by Todd and Tony Hensley, thank you for this splendid show, contest, and catalog.

I am particularly grateful to those C&T professionals who worked most closely on this book: Liz Aneloski, my editor, who documented the quilts and oversaw the organization of the catalog; Sara MacFarland, my technical editor whose accountability and attention to detail are increasingly rare treasures; Diane Pedersen, Director of Production, whose delight in overseeing the book's visual impact shows in joyous results; Adrianne Shroyer, who has kept the careful records and administered the contest, and Micaela Carr the book designer who has brought this catalog to life.

We at C&T Publishing thank Peter and David Mancuso, proprietors of the annual Pacific International Quilt Show, for providing a superb forum here in Santa Clara for our Baltimore Album Revival Show.

Thank you to our fine jury and to our judges, Mary Leman Austin, Editorial Director of Quilter's® Newsletter Magazine, and Nadine Thompson, teacher, lecturer, and 1996 Best of Show winner in the "Revival of a Classic Style" Category. By gift of their time and talent, they honor us all.

Our thanks and appreciation go to our magnanimous 1998 show sponsors for their tangible support and for their share in this communal celebration.

Show Sponsors

P&B TEXTILES

QUILTER'S NEWSLETTER MAGAZINE

BERNINA®

Fairfield

Quilters' Resource®

FISKARS®

©1998 Eleanor Patton Hamilton Sienkiewicz
Editor: Liz Aneloski
Technical Editor: Sara Kate MacFarland
Copy Editor: Vera Tobin
Design Director: Diane Pedersen
Cover and Book Designer: Micaela Miranda Carr
Photographer: Kathleen Bellesiles ©C&T Publishing, Inc. unless otherwise noted
ISBN: 1-57120-046-0

The Baltimore clipper ship on the front cover is a block from *Embellishing Baltimore*. Full quilt pictured on page 17. Details on back cover are from *The Blossoms of Baltimore*, this page, and *Made in California*, page 22.

Sienkiewicz, Elly.
    Baltimore album legacy / Elly Sienkiewicz.
        p.   cm.
    "Catalog of C&T Publishing's Baltimore album revival quilt show and contest; Pacific International Quilt Show, Santa Clara, CA, October 8-11, 1998."
        ISBN 1-57120-046-0 (pbk.)
        1. Album quilts—Maryland—Baltimore—Exhibitions.
I. C&T Publishing.   II. Title.
NK9112.S54   1998
746.46'074794'73—dc21   98-24727
                                                      CIP

Baltimore Beauties is a trademark of Elly Sienkiewicz.
Pigma Micron is a registered trademark of Sakura Color Products.

Published by C&T Publishing, Inc., P.O. Box 1456, Lafayette, California 94549
Printed in Hong Kong

10   9   8   7   6   5   4   3   2   1

103. THE BLOSSOMS OF BALTIMORE

CAROLYN SUSAC
Reno, Nevada
60" x 60"

Judges

Contest

C&T Publishing's first Baltimore Album Revival Exhibition stunned its audience. Time had been, not two decades ago, when no one imagined that late 20th century quiltmakers could approach the antebellum Baltimores in conceptual ambition, diligence of construction, virtuosity of needlework, evocative imagery, or soul-searing beauty. Each such treasured quilt antiquity, like the pyramids of old, was considered a never-to-be-rivaled artifact. When, in 1994, more than 100 contemporary Album-style quilts hung at C&T's first show, the Revivalists' eloquence echoed that of the old ones. The entries could not and did not even try to reproduce specific antique quilts. With silent passion, they witnessed that a classic needleart expression had been relearned in all its intricacies of design and execution. A genre of Revivalist Baltimores had been made by women whose lives and times in unexpected ways so resembled those of 150 years ago, when Baltimore Albums were first in bloom. The old gave voice to the new.

In the 1994 Contest, the largest category into which quilts were entered was the "Revival of a Classic Style." Even there, with its call to adhere to tradition, one could sense in the details a contemporary style evolving. Quiltmakers stitched their own lives and times and brought their own aesthetic tastes to the task. This contemporary sparkle said "today!" and shared stylistic innovations—that which qualifies our quiltmaking as still a folk art—identified a renaissance. While the Revival was witnessed in the first show, a heightened expectation of evolution "Beyond Baltimore" generated this second show. "Baltimore," a style at first so intimidating to modern quiltmakers, has once again come fully into its own, here at the turn of the 20th century. To celebrate the role of Elly's Baltimore Beauties® series in sustaining the breadth and evolution of this Revivalist Baltimore style, C&T Publishers invited two quilt luminaries to join Elly in judging the show. We are delighted that they accepted the invitation.

The Judges

MARY LEMAN AUSTIN, EDITORIAL DIRECTOR, QUILTER'S NEWSLETTER MAGAZINE

Since Mary's parents, Bonnie and George Leman, began *Quilter's Newsletter Magazine* in 1969, it has chronicled and inspired the current quiltmaking revival. *Quilter's Newsletter* remains—as its name implies—a vital cord, binding quiltmakers together into an enthusiastic, and incredibly productive world-wide sub-culture. When Bonnie retired, Mary was asked to take on the position of Editor-in-Chief. Subscribers welcomed Mary in this role since she had been an integral part of *QNM* since day one when she herself was just 13 years old.

Early on, Mary became the pattern drafter and illustrator for the young publication, then managed Art and Production for many years. Half a dozen years ago she was, in addition, asked to take on an editorial re-design for *Quiltmaker*, *QNM's* sister publication. "It was like being given a magazine to run with." But she enjoyed the move to Editorial and is now most identifiably visible in her opening letter under the rubric "Needle Notes".

Mary's quiltmaking runs to traditional block-style quilts presented with a fresh twist. As editor-in-chief, daughter, sibling, wife, and aunt in a large and growing family, Mary particularly enjoys the occasional time when she needs to do a quilt design for an issue. A year or so ago *QNM* ran a thoughtful series on quilt judging. Mary confesses herself to be of mixed minds on the issue of judging, seeing in it both positive and negative potential. It is just that sort of thoughtful weighing of all sides of an issue that make her participation as a judge in this contest so valued. Then, back in the everyday quilt world where life is truly lived, we will look forward to reading Mary's thoughts, getting to know her in a quiet moment, and smiling inwardly as we receive her affectionate editorial fare-thee-well, "Until next month, Happy Quilting."

AUTHOR UNDERLININGS & MARGINALIA

Nothing that is worth doing can be achieved in our lifetime; therefore we must be saved by hope. Nothing which is true or beautiful or good makes complete sense in any immediate context of history; therefore we must be saved by faith. Nothing we do, however virtuous, can be accomplished alone; therefore we must be saved by love.
—Reinhold Niebuhr

AUTHOR'S NOTE

Does every hard-wrought Baltimore reflect faith, hope, and love? To the extent that the viewer perceives this, does that quilt have magic? A power over the human spirit?

Philosophy

The Quilt Show Philosophy

AUTHOR UNDERLININGS & MARGINALIA

What moves men of genius, or rather what inspires their work, is not new ideas, but their obsession with the idea that what has already been said is still not enough.
—Eugene Delacroix

AUTHOR'S NOTE

The classic Baltimores gave us a language, a format, a way to express our own lives.

NADINE THOMPSON, PRIZE-WINNING QUILTMAKER, DESIGNER, TEACHER, LECTURER

When noting the number of Baltimore-style Album Quilts originating just beyond California's Bay Area, look among them for Nadine Thompson's influence. For some twelve years now, Nadine has been teaching quilt-related classes both in the area's shops and guilds and nationally. Previously, she worked for eight years in new product development for the Sunset Designs art needlework company. As long as 30 years ago her needlework won awards, but in recent years her most prestigious kudos have come for her quilts.

To see Nadine's *Baltimore Memories* (Best of Show, Revival of a Classic Style, BAR I Contest 1996) is to know something important about its maker. The quilt seems perfect in all respects—color, cloth, proportion, dynamics of the set, grace and suitability of the border, and unifying all, the exquisite workmanship of a careful and devoted quiltmaker. The quilt evolved slowly as Nadine learned, then taught, block by block, a full repertoire of Baltimore-style techniques. As a dedicated quiltmaker will, she stitched in those things she cherishes most, those attachments and memories which give the viewer intimations of soul. Like life itself, Nadine had certain "givens" at each stage and made her quilt's journey into a masterpiece of beauty.

The dedication which enabled Nadine to undertake, and then complete, a quilt in this complex style, to meld all those disparate elements into a unified whole; the artist's eye which set together individual blocks; the patient care of her fine workmanship; the pristine orderliness of the finished piece: one perceives all these qualities in *Baltimore Memories*. We are grateful that she brings these to help judge this contest.

Some classic Album Quilts going for six-figure prices at art and antique auctions of the 1980s and '90s might not be allowed to win Best of Show in a contemporary contest, because many popular judging standards today rely most heavily on quantifiable qualities. Such judging philosophies tend to overvalue a checklist of specific technical details rather than seeing the whole as greater than the sum of its parts. Reviving the antique appliqué Album Quilts appeals widely to quiltmakers of diverse talents and inclinations—people who see and express life differently. The judges' goal is to commend a particularly personal and expressive beauty, the sort which makes a quilt most memorable. The judges will ask: Does the quilt inspire, give a sense of its maker, uplift with its beauty? If the answer is yes, then its workmanship succeeds. But no quilt shall be devalued for technical details which do not detract from the quilt's overall impression and power upon the viewer. We seek to reward for timeless qualities, for the quilt's dynamism as a work of art. Because our show philosophy is to look for an indefinable beauty, a sort of "magic" if you will, a judge will not write comments on a quilt's technical details unless moved to do so.

In the end, judging is just that: a best-effort, considered opinion of individuals first, then of consensus reached among the three judges in the time allotted. Each judge will present a Judge's Choice to reward a quilt which she loved but which did not finish among the consensus winners. While the majority—wonderful quilts all—won't receive special mention, to all who offered to share their masterpieces through this show, C&T Publishing commends your generosity with the greatest of admiration, noting: *Each of these Album Quilts, even those not juried into the show, is truly a winner—now and for posterity.* With enviable passion and artistry, each quiltmaker has given new life to a classic and particularly expressive quilt style. Thank you for entering the show, and thank you for bringing appliqué Albums to such glorious bloom again in the late-20th century. Thank you for taking "Baltimore" so beautifully "beyond".

ELLY SIENKIEWICZ, AUTHOR,
Baltimore Beauties and Beyond Series

TODD HENSLEY, PRESIDENT,
C&T Publishing, Inc.

Categories

Contest Categories

I. BEAUTIFULLY INNOVATIVE (sponsored by Quilter's Newsletter Magazine): The award for Beautifully Innovative is given in recognition of a quilt, which takes the classic Baltimore style beautifully "beyond".

II. REVIVAL OF A CLASSIC STYLE (sponsored by P&B Textiles): A classic style is first learned and its principles understood by faithful reproduction. The award for Revival of a Classic Style applauds this accomplishment.

III. REFLECTIVE OF PARTICULAR LIVES AND TIMES (sponsored by Fiskars® Manufacturing Corporation): Elly once wrote that these quilts were "a window into the soul of the women who made them." The award for Reflective of Particular Lives and Times is given for a quilt particularly expressive of the maker or of the person or theme the quilt was designed to commemorate.

Awards

Special Awards

BEST OF SHOW: MADE PREDOMINANTLY BY HAND (sponsored by Fairfield Processing Corporation): Deemed Best of Show by a consensus of the judges, this award commends the Revivalist Baltimore Album-style Quilt done predominantly by hand.

BEST OF SHOW: MADE PREDOMINANTLY BY MACHINE (sponsored by Bernina® of America): Deemed Best of Show by a consensus of the judges, this award commends the Revivalist Baltimore Album-style Quilt done predominantly by machine.

JUDGE'S CHOICE AWARD (sponsored by C&T Publishing): Each judge will have an opportunity to reward a quilt she considers particularly worthy but which has not already won a prize.

LOUISE O. TOWNSEND MEMORIAL AWARD (sponsored by C&T Publishing): C&T Publishing will present the award for its favorite Baltimore Album-style Quilt in honor of the late Louise O. Townsend who edited many of the books in Elly's *Baltimore Beauties and Beyond* series.

DIMENSIONAL FLOWERS AWARD (sponsored by Quilters' Resource): By consensus of the judges, this award shall be given to the quiltmaker who best incorporates dimensional floral motifs into her quilt.

HONORED TEACHER (sponsored by C&T Publishing.): C&T honors each teacher of the Baltimore style who has made it bloom so gloriously once again in her own region. We asked students to tell how a teacher has affected their work and the work of others in their area. The Honored Teacher Award is given to the teacher who received the greatest number of nominations from admiring students.

Carol Baker of Wisconsin
Shirley Brabson of New Mexico
Anne Connery of Maryland
Audrey Derscha of Michigan
Dixie Haywood of Florida
Anne Morrison of Manitoba, Canada
Marlene Peterman of California
Betty Rieck of Iowa
Laurene Sinema of Arizona
Louisa Smith of Massachusetts
Nadine Thompson of California
Laurie Toensing of Minnesota
Albertine Veenstra of Massachusetts
Alice Wilhoit of Texas

AUTHOR
UNDERLININGS &
MARGINALIA

[Artists] have to forge a character subtle enough to nourish and protect and foster the growth of the part of themselves that makes art, and at the same time practical enough to deal with the world pragmatically.

They have to maintain a position between care of themselves and care of their work in the world…
—Anne Truitt,
DayBook, The Journal of An Artist

AUTHOR'S NOTE

Today's younger quilt-making women most often say, "I like hand appliqué because it's portable. I can stitch at meetings, or while I'm waiting to pick up my children. I can do it in the evening and be with my family."

Legacy

The Baltimore Album Legacy, Briefly

The Baltimore Album style is a complex style, one that has immediate visual impact, but one which also richly rewards closer inspection. The richest classic Baltimore Album Quilts raise questions, have an air of mystery, and intrigue us into diverse roads of inquiry. This tension enlightens us, not in the modern way of pat answers and data-based arguments, but in a transcendent way that leaves us open to broader understandings.

The fanciest antebellum Baltimores (1845-55) dazzle with lifelike draftsmanship, evocative fabric, and half-forgotten iconographies. The mid-19th century's ornate Baltimore Album Quilt style might have been an historic flash of genius, but became instead a classic. Its popularity bespeaks a movement, one which flourished for a decade or so in Baltimore, then spread far north and west of the city which had spawned it. We moderns inherited hundreds of related Album Quilts—all so mysterious in origin, each so fascinating in feature. In a little-analyzed reincarnation, this style is now born again in the late 20th century. It has taken wider hold than its ancestor, gaining followers to the north in Canada; east to European capitals, on to American expatriates in Saudi Arabia, and further to Japan and Korea; south to South Africa, Australia, and New Zealand. Now, in the second decade of this revival, Baltimore style has developed its own recognizably late-20th-century characteristics. We call this contemporary-style Album Quilt a "Revivalist Baltimore."

Confluent forces shaped Revivalist Baltimores. Back in 1983 *Spoken Without a Word* met the initial challenge by reproducing antique Baltimore block patterns and probing the secrets of their symbols. By *Baltimore Beauties and Beyond, Volume I*, it was more than enough simply to rediscover the basics of stitching classic Baltimore Album style appliqué. There, large-scale prints are often paired with papercut appliqués. This initially was an innovative practice but now characterizes Revivalist Baltimores. Because the Album style offered a challenge and satisfied a hunger, it caught on. *Dimensional Appliqué* (1994), for example, firmly

inserted ribbon into the changing style. As the Baltimore Beauties series grew, so did communal knowledge of the style. The women and times that had cradled the original Album Quilts became familiar. As was the case for women of that era, the winds of political and social change leave us feeling less in control of our lives. We discover an affinity: the more we understand those ladies, the better we understand ourselves. These sensibilities, coupled with our burgeoning mastery of appliqué, have set us free. It is as though we moderns are admiring daughters, come finally into our own womanhood. Emulating our "mothers" we stitch our own lives into expressive Album Quilts, proudly evoking their heritage. Occasionally a modern Album is so reminiscent of an elder that it brings tears to the eyes, as though a classic quilt has been reborn through a living soul. At other times, only we who know and love the old ones can detect the family's genes in a Revivalist Album, so different does the new one look.

Enjoined to compose an essay for *Baltimore Album Legacy,* I considered summarizing this renaissance. To be frank, though, I have no desire to name the epoch come and gone, for it is but newly in full bloom. Too many love too much the path "Baltimore" has set them on, find the Baltimore style too vital, too suited to our lives here in the late 20th century, too fascinating and all-encompassing not to continue on where this journey is leading them. Beginning Baltimore classes fill across the country while some long on this journey stitch on their "Baltimore" intermittently, savoring its evolution. Rare women (Marian Brockschmidt, Cleda Dawson, Ardeth Laake, and Nancy Welsch among them) have made six and more intricate "Baltimores." Some stitch their second or third Revivalist Album, while others make one square at a time, enjoying the process and in no hurry to finish. In public forums, Revivalist Baltimores—each more compelling than the last—have in recent years taken top prize at the world's most prestigious quilt competitions. This bespeaks an appreciative public and a current fluency in stitchery techniques and symbolic tongues.

The Baltimore Revival raises questions whose answers one can only intuit: Why are Baltimore-style Album Quilts born again—now? In what ways does getting to know the Classic Baltimores nourish us? What loneliness or longing does it lessen? Might Revivalist Album Quiltmaking serve a connective function? (It connects Album makers into a recognizable sub-culture as much as it connects Album quilters from one century to the next. It integrates the quiltmaker's life as she recalls loved ones, records memories, and selects meaningful inscriptions. It helps us comprehend life's mysteries, answer unanswerable questions, work out contradictions which haunt us. Its ritual takes one on a transformational journey.) Much is said these days about attending to our spiritual needs. Is Album-making in part a spiritual activity? This Exhibition's visual feast will provide some answers. In addition, this catalog's written selections address our wonderment in an experiential manner. First, the "Author's Underlinings and Marginalia" traces my own fascination with pondering these matters. The second excerpt is from my journal after I'd spent the day judging a major international quilt show. In the *art spirit,* may this writing blend with the images of Album Quilts on exhibition. In the words of Robert Henri, the art spirit's "subject is beauty—or happiness, and man's approach to it is various."

sound is seamless and a bit too loud. But its throb is exhilarating, like city lights and crowds of people moving as though on mechanical sidewalks, at rush hour. The light here is unfamiliar: low floodlights set the occasional landscaped tree aglow from the ground up. Cottony clouds reflect the nighttime city's pinkish aura and slip by, moving almost imperceptibly against a charcoaled sky. Strings of diamond-bright lights draw electric building outlines while here and there a window glows warm yellow through billowing drapes.

It is after dark, yet the night is alive with unfamiliar lights and sounds. And I am a bit lonely, a solitary quilter come to an international quilt gathering halfway across the country. This elegant hotel is a hollow stack of guest floors with a sunken lounge in the center; a trio is now playing beside the bar and cocktail waitresses attend the throng of guests. Though I would surely know some people there, I shied away at the thought of entering that crowd alone and have instead come to sit awhile in the cool, in the dark, by the pool. "Excuse me, m'am," says the young man whom I'd noticed out of the corner of my eye. He is the

AUTHOR
UNDERLININGS &
MARGINALIA

Meditation in a state of activity is a thousand times more profound than that in a state of quietude.
—*Daie, 9th century Zen master*

AUTHOR'S NOTE

Can quilting be meditation?

121.
CEILTEACH CIRCLES

CATHY GRAFTON
Pontiac, Illinois
74" x 74"

Passion...

These Are the Quilts that Make You Cry

NOTES FROM A JUDGE'S JOURNAL
HOUSTON, TEXAS, OCTOBER 26, 1995

To judge a major quilt show is an honor. It is also a responsibility borne seriously. And it is hard work. Yesterday I judged such a show and upon returning, fell asleep in my hotel room without a pause for supper. Tomorrow, I will walk over to the George R. Brown Convention center and in the Quilt Festival Office there, sign those American International Quilt Guild prize ribbons which I have awarded. Tonight I am sitting on my window balcony beside the sixth floor pool deck of the Hyatt Regency. The air is a tease, dancing with my scarf and patting my cheeks, pushing at my hair, and riffling the water. Ceaseless bar music plays over the October-empty blue pool: the

AUTHOR UNDERLININGS & MARGINALIA

To know what you prefer instead of humbly saying Amen to what the world tells you you ought to prefer, is to have kept your soul alive.
—Robert Louis Stevenson

What we play is life.
—Louis Armstrong

What is all this juice and all this joy?
—Gerard Manley Hopkins (1844-89)

As to me, I know of nothing else but miracles.
—Walt Whitman

[Walt Whitman's] work is an autobiography-not of haps and mishaps, but of his deepest thought, his life indeed.
—Robert Henri

AUTHOR'S NOTE

Each hard-wrought quilt is an autobiography. But it is in the very nature of Revivalist Albums specifically to *intend* autobiography.

deck's other sole occupant, taking a smoke and an evening walk. "Were you out here last night? That building over there was all lit up with green and red neon lights. It was so pretty. I wondered what it was." I answer in a friendly, but older-lady-cautious way. He is a solidly built tow-head, clean-shaven and in his twenties. In the dark his black and white striped jersey is more visible than his face. He has moved on, but I sensed that he was lonely, too, as we are wont to be when we are away from home.

I am thinking now of the quilt show, of the lives stitched into those quilts, of the degree of intimacy revealed, or of the feelings hardly touched upon. Some quilts were light-hearted and quick, others were intellectual and almost art-school perfect. But certain quilts held you as though in communion with another soul. In their stillness, they spoke: one could feel echoed the still, sad music of humanity. But more; for some rare quilts offered the gift of a life full enough with hard-come faith to share wisdom with another fellow; to share it even with a generation yet unborn. I don't really mean a rote religious faith or even necessarily something one can put into words. One senses the faith of someone who has lived life deeply, who has seen its dark side, but who never falters in putting life's puzzle pieces into a positive picture.

We were four judges for four hundred quilts. Our day had begun with a 7:15 a.m. breakfast. The quilts were divided into categories so that each judge looked at some one hundred quilts. A scribe assisted each one of us, recording our careful comments quilt by quilt, then, as they were completed, taking each judge's top prize winners to the head scribe. By 4:00 p.m. we congregated to choose the Best of Show large quilt and the Best of Show small quilt from among the first prize winners in each category. The convention center was almost empty now, save for us judges and the four hundred quilts. Tomorrow it would be a hive of activity generated by the merchants and manufacturers setting up for Quilt Market, the quilt world's wholesale show. By next week's end, more than 50,000 people are expected to have come to see the quilts. Gratefully, we accepted the offer to be driven on a golf cart to review the rows of quilts. Each judge pointed out the top winner for her categories. The small quilt Best of

Show was quickly agreed upon: It was a fiber art piece, exceptionally well done.

By sheer number, competition was stiffer among the large quilts, for a large quilt may require more of the self than a small quilt, and the sheer magnitude of effort may result in a higher achievement. Our final choice was not easy, but the comments that lead up to it were revealing. The top prize winners seemed of two characters: On the one hand were stunning quilts, quilts embodying an idea conceived and carefully worked out in colored cloth, painstakingly arranged, then carefully stitched through with patterned quilting. The level of art throughout the show was breathtaking, as though world-class museum treasures had nothing on these modern quiltmakers' talent, creativity, diligence, and high standards. On the other hand were quilts perhaps a tad less perfectly wrought in quantifiable ways, yet they took one's breath away. This second group of top contenders had some quality much harder to name.

One judge said, "Those other quilts are perfect designs, fabric art, intellectual triumphs. But these two are the kind of quilt that makes you cry." We had, all four, come back finally to one of the two. It was an Album Quilt, softly colored, yet lively and full of the stuff of life: Tiny bell-shaped blossoms hung on fragile stems, a life-size ladybug crawled up a stem to peek into a bud, a maternal blue bird alighted on her nest. And cradled by that bordering generosity of nature were man's ancient offerings of music from a lyre, and woven baskets to hold the blessings and the wonder. Though only nine blocks, each sang such a song of silent praise as to lift the hearts of we beholders.

One of my fellow judges laughed gently to herself. "Yes, this one's clearly it. It will be good to see it pulled out from the others and shown in the light, focused upon as it deserves. Everyone will say 'Elly had such power that a Baltimore-style Album has won 'the Best of Show,' but this quilt simply is the winner.'"

"No." I heard myself saying softly, "It is the quilt. You can feel the maker's passion. This is the kind of quilt that makes you want to cry."

Each judge is allowed a ribbon to give for whatever reason she chooses. I gave my judge's choice ribbon to a beautifully unique quilt called *Ancient Stories* [by Charlotte Patera]. From dramatically saturated batiks, aboriginal figures and symbols had been reverse appliquéd in a hotly colored primitive dance. The appliqué was neatly done by hand: one could feel the maker's pleasure in it. She chose deep, emphatic lines of machine quilting as the perfect finish, stitching ancient to modern firmly, and with a flourish. I would love to have that quilt, to own it: I liked its aesthetics, I like that it ties us to what has made us what we are. It is an object of art which speaks to me and breaks a smile from my soul. As for the Best of Show quilt, I would love just to hug its maker, for through her beautiful quilt, she shared the gift of her own faith and hope and love. It seemed a gift shyly, but freely, given to we who viewed her quilt. Now I have her gift for all my days of joy and sorrow. Thank you, Ellen Heck. I'll turn in now, knowing that I'll face tomorrow's challenges with courage renewed.

AUTHOR
UNDERLININGS &
MARGINALIA

Painting is just another way of keeping a diary.
—Pablo Picasso

The creation of something new is not accomplished by the intellect but by the play instinct acting from inner necessity. The creative mind plays with the objects it loves.
—Carl. G. Jung

AUTHOR'S NOTE

In Album-making, technical mastery frees the play instinct.

405.
BALTIMORE
COUNTRY

FRANCES ABELL
BRAND
West Dennis,
Massachusetts
68" x 68"

Photo: Jeffrey D. Hetler

429. BALTIMORE COMES TO THE PRAIRIE

PRAIRIE QUILT GUILD
Wichita, Kansas
93" x 108"

108. BALTIMORE SHADES OF SUMMER

DANIELLE BROUWER-NABER
Uden, The Netherlands
61½" x 61½"

420. ALBUM OF FRIENDSHIP

DEBRA BALLARD
Midland, Michigan
81½" x 81½"

104. LOVE'S ASPECTS

CAROL WIGHT JONES
Puyallup, Washington
72" x 78"

700. THE FRIENDSHIP, LOVE, AND TRUTH QUILT

KATHRYN F. TENNYSON
Chestertown, New York
80" x 92"

Photo: Rick Rhodes

107. A BALTIMORE ADVENTURE— FLORA & FAUNA

RUTH H. MCIVER
Johns Island, South Carolina
88½" x 89½"

Photo: Andrew Payne

421. QUILT FOR ELOISE

JUDY BONNER
North Richmond, NSW, Australia
83" x 83"

16

713. The Lady's Red Hat

Phyllis A. Street
Honaker, Virginia
82" x 82"

113. EMBELLISHING BALTIMORE

JENIFER BUECHEL
Library, Pennsylvania
80" x 80"

18

Photo: Masaaki Takegami

102. HANA—1007

Yumiko Hirasawa
Tsuzuki-ku, Yokohama, Japan
73½" x 85"

112. An English Cottage
Garden...Stolen Moments
in the Garden

Faye Labanaris
Dover, New Hampshire
88" x 78"

Photo: Thom Hindle

430. KINDAMO FAMILY ALBUM

CORINE BUECHNER
Marcell, Minnesota
90" x 90"

Photo: Julia Brook-White

411. FAMILY ALBUM QUILT

MARGERY MCCARTHY
Taupo, New Zealand
80" x 92½"

119. BALTIMORE NIGHTS

SHERRY LOEFFLER
Port Townsend, Washington
97" x 97"

704. CARMEL BY THE SEA ALBUM

JEANNIE OLIVERIA
Pacific Grove, California
75" x 90"

124. A HAUNTED CASTLE
IN BALTIMORE

LYNNE BOWBEER
Saline, Michigan
104" x 104"

415. MADE IN CALIFORNIA

NANCY BUSBY
Rio Vista, California
92" x 92"

402. Blest Be the Ties that Bind

Cape Cod Chapter of the
Good Ladies of Baltimore
Dennis Massachusetts
70 x 82½"

**117. Homage to Jane
Stickle and Mary Evans**

Brenda Papadakis
Indianapolis, Indiana
quilted by Cathy Franks
77" x 92"

407. BALTIMORE ALBUM

DARLENE SCOW
Salt Lake City, Utah
84" x 84"

110. REFLECTIONS OF THE GARDEN

SUSAN K. COOK
Coshocton, Ohio
80" x 80"

Photo: William Brockschmidt Photography

408. BALTIMORE BLOOMS IN 3-D

MARIAN K. BROCKSCHMIDT
Springfield, Illinois
72" x 72"

410. TO KELLY WITH LOVE

JUDI ROBB
Manhattan, Kansas
83" x 83"

409. BALTIMORE ROSE

SHARON FLUECKINGER
Rapid City, South Dakota
76½" x 99½"

Photo: Mark Gulelian

708. SUSAN'S SERENITY

SUSAN E. HINZMAN
Bethesda, Maryland
91" x 91"

116. KAW VALLEY FLORAL BOUQUET

KAW VALLEY QUILTERS GUILD
Lawrence, Kansas
86" x 92"

705. LITTLE BROWN BIRD

MARGARET DOCHERTY
Durham, United Kingdon
84" x 84½"

428. BALTIMORE BLOOMS II

ANN HOLDEN PLUMMER
Pleasanton, California
90" x 90"

Photo: Art Wiebe

404. BALTIMORE ALBUM BEAUTIE

PEARL BRAUN DYCK
Plum Coulee, Manitoba, Canada
90½" x 90½"

414. MOMMA'S GONNA BUY YOU A MOCKING BIRD

PATRICIA C. LUCEY
Boxford, Massachusetts
80" x 80"

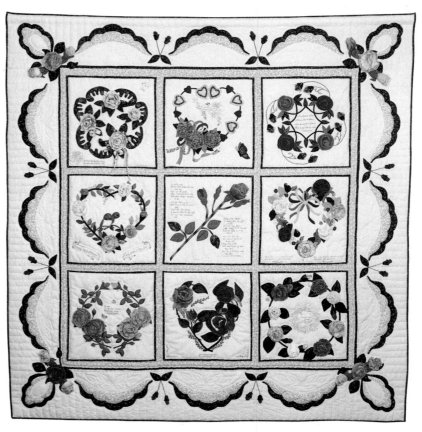

Photo: Bret Hanwright

128. GO LOVELY ROSE

BALTIMORE ALBUM FRIENDS GROUP
Kingaroy, Queensland, Australia
58" x 58"

Category #1

BEAUTIFULLY INNOVATIVE

Sponsored by Quilter's Newsletter Magazine

100
ROSE WREATHED BOUQUET
ARDETH J. LAAKE
Bemond, Iowa
64" x 64", 1995 to 1996
Medallion quilt made of 100% cotton fabrics, silk ribbon, suede cloth, and Pigma® pen inking. Sixth Baltimore album to be made for a grandchild. Appliqué and reverse appliqué techniques used, as well as hand quilting with cotton batting.

101
GERRI'S SALVATION
GERRI REYNOLDS
Mercer, Wisconsin
94" x 102", 1994 to 1998
During rehabilitation after a severe leg injury Gerri hand appliquéd and hand quilted sixteen-block quilt from 100% cotton fabrics. Each square reminds her that one small stitch after another can create something worthwhile—as one small step after another could help her walk again. Family names in border blocks of this work-in-progress; leaving space for yet-to-be-born grandchildren and great-grandchildren.

102
HANA—1007
Photo on page 18
YUMIKO HIRASAWA
Tsuzuki-ku, Yokohama, Japan
73½" x 85", 1997
Thirty-block quilt made to convey to Yumiko's son and the children of the future that it is our responsibility to protect and cherish the clear sky, clean ocean, colorful flowers, and other forms of life that inhabit this world. The original-design border gives the look of twisted lace and string and combines with appliqué and papercut blocks.

103
THE BLOSSOMS OF BALTIMORE
Photo on page 2
CAROLYN SUSAC
Reno, Nevada
quilted by Clara Smith
60" x 60", 1997 to 1998
Medallion-style quilt made from hand-dyed 100% cotton fabrics, dimensional flowers, and original-design leaves and border. Quilt made from a combination of friendship, shared ideas, and the design elements mainly of the ladies who made the original classic Baltimore album quilts.

104
LOVE'S ASPECTS
Photo on page 15
CAROL WIGHT JONES
Puyallup, Washington
72" x 78", 1992 to 1997
While appliquéing nine heart blocks, Carol pondered various aspects of love the hearts represented. Several of most meaningful aspects are inscribed in heart centers using Pigma pen. Heart sashing continues theme, followed by Dancing Grapevine border and echo quilting.

105
PACIFIC GROVE ALBUM
Photo on page 21
JEANNIE OLIVERIA
Pacific Grove, California
86" x 102", 1994 to 1996
Twenty-block quilt made out of love for her hometown, includes historical renderings and hand appliqué and quilting. Album quilting fulfills verse in Jeannie's life: "Make it your ambition to lead a quiet and peaceful life, and to work with your hands." I Thes. 4:11

Art in community has a subtle, unconscious, refining influence.
— Robert Henri

106
LEAP YEAR IN THE LOWVELD
PAT PARKER AND JENNY WILLIAMSON
Bordeaux, South Africa
60" x 74", 1995
African adaptation of Baltimore album quilt. Pat's and Jenny's love for wilderness area in South Africa called the Lowveld inspired images of rural people in colorful apparel and an abundance of indigenous flora and fauna. Appliqué and sashing worked in vibrant colors and unusual vital printed designs of Africa. In keeping with African art, blocks are designed in a naive manner. Embellished with embroidery and shadow quilted.

107
A BALTIMORE ADVENTURE—FLORA & FAUNA
Photo on page 13
RUTH H. MCIVER
Johns Island, South Carolina
88½" x 89½", 1993 to 1995

Medallion-style quilt reflects many aspects of Ruth's life in the country on Johns Island, SC: animals and birds she enjoys viewing from her windows, yard, and pasture. Border inspired by grape vines that grow in the yard. Quilt made as a result of Ruth's appreciation and admiration of style and artistry of old Baltimore quilts.

108
BALTIMORE SHADES OF SUMMER
Photo on page 12
DANIELLE BROUWER-NABER
Uden, The Netherlands
61½" x 61½", 1997 to 1998
Danielle wanted the quilt to be very colorful, so chose golden-yellow for background rather than usual cream color. Quilt was started in Texas and completed in The Netherlands. Hand appliqué and quilting were used with 100% cotton fabrics and cotton/polyester batting.

109

BALTIMORE BASKETS,
VASES AND WREATHS
JUDY SCHWARZMANN
Concord, California
79" x 94", 1994
Twenty-block quilt made using hand
appliqué, silk ribbon, beading, and
acrylic ribbon, with inscriptions
meaningful to Judy. Quilt was
a turning point in Judy's quiltmaking. She now does only appliqué
and almost always designs her own
quilts or changes designs to make
them her own.

110

REFLECTIONS OF THE GARDEN
Photo on page 25
SUSAN K. COOK
Coshocton, Ohio
80" x 80", 1993 to 1995
Quilt began with idea of reflecting
beauty of Susan's backyard perennial
garden flowers, but came to reflect
much more. Cotton and silk fabrics
from Malaysia and Europe were used
for the blocks with appliqué and three-
dimensional work. Susan's favorite
flower, as well as her mother's, is the
rose—thus the use of roses. Hobbes
black batt was used in this hand-
appliquéd, hand-quilted piece.

111

NATURE'S BEAUTY
PAULA CARTER
Plano, Texas
quilted by Laura Schwartz
65" x 75", 1994 to 1998
Center medallion quilt incorporates two
of Paula's loves: flowers and birds. Wired
silk ribbon, embroidery floss, 100% cotton fabrics and hand-dyed fabrics used
for the appliqué and trapunto, finished
by hand-quilted cross-hatching.

Be still and cool in thy
own mind and spirit.
— George Fox, Quaker theologian

112

AN ENGLISH COTTAGE GARDEN...
STOLEN MOMENTS IN THE GARDEN
Photo on page 18
FAYE LABANARIS
Dover, New Hampshire
88" x 78", 1997 to 1998
Faye's love of flowers, beauty of
English cottage gardens, and British
countryside inspired her to create
contemporary set of classic Baltimore
blocks using floral chintz fabrics, metallic
threads, and dimensional flowers of
French ribbon. Inked cottage and
garden bordered with floral chintz fabric.
Tribute to Princess Diana is included
with inked scroll containing words to
"Candle in the Wind."

113

EMBELLISHING BALTIMORE
Photo on cover and page 17
JENIFER BUECHEL
Library, Pennsylvania
80" x 80", 1997 to 1998
Nine-block quilt includes 100% cotton
fabrics, hand-dyed silk and ribbon,
beading, decorative embroidery, inkings,
stuffed work, metallic braid, brass
findings, and gold lamé.

114

SASKATOON AT NOON IN JUNE
DIANNE DOUGLAS
Saskatoon, Canada
64" x 64", 1995
Dianne's first appliqué quilt, meant to
reflect exuberance and joy of a summer
day in beautiful prairie city of Saskatoon.
Cotton, silk, and ultrasuede fabrics
manipulated with hand appliqué, hand
and machine embroidery, inking, stuffed
work, machine guided quilting, and
machine trapunto.

115

MAY FLOWERS
MICHELLE JANE HUDDLESTON
Pittsburg, California
63" x 63", 1993 to 1998
Twentieth anniversary quilt made
using hand appliqué and hand quilting,
stipple quilting, and machine piecing
with 100% cotton fabrics. Most blocks
inscribed with brown Pigma pen.

Michelle is a self-taught quilter once
intimidated by the appliqué process.

116

KAW VALLEY FLORAL BOUQUET
Photo on page 10
KAW VALLEY QUILTERS GUILD
Lawrence, Kansas
86" x 92", 1997
Quilt designed by Shirley and Shirlene
Wedd. Hand appliquéd, hand pieced,
machine appliquéd, and hand quilted by
guild members using 100% cotton fabric
and batting. Native Kansas fruits and
flowers and the Kaw Valley Quilters
Guild logo, the sunflower, were the
inspiration for the quilt. By including
grapes, sunflowers, trumpetvine and
thistle, a broad color palette was created,
making a vibrant and unique quilt.

117

HOMAGE TO JANE STICKLE AND
MARY EVANS
Photo on page 23
BRENDA PAPADAKIS
Indianapolis, Indiana
quilted by Cathy Franks
77" x 92", 1996 to 1998
Quilt is marriage of two different
concepts in quilting: one attributed to
Mary Evans with soft floral designs
found in traditional Baltimore album
quilts; the other evolves from geometric
designs in Jane Stickle's 1863 Civil War
quilt. Quilt is fashioned around piece
of fabric Brenda's husband bought in
France and represents their love,
marriage, and merging of two cultures,
Greek and American.

118

BRIGHTEN THE CORNER
MARJORIE HAIGHT LYDECKER
Dennis, Massachusetts
79" x 79", 1997
Nine-block quilt made for one of
Marjorie's children. Rather than remov-
ing the original appliquéd pieces the
color of which didn't blend properly as
quilt progressed, Marjorie appliquéd a
second, different colored fabric over
some of the original flowers and leaves.
Hand quilted.

119
BALTIMORE NIGHTS
Photo on page 20
SHERRY LOEFFLER
Port Townsend, Washington
97" x 97", 1995 to 1998
Quilt was made for pure pleasure, using cotton and cotton/polyester blend fabrics with gray polyester batting, and using hand appliqué and quilting techniques. Instead of using a light background and bright colors, Sherry chose to use a black background and pastel colors for her diagonally set quilt.

120
*MEGAN'S MENAGERIE OF
RIBBONS & ROSES*
DEBRA BALLARD
Midland, Michigan
quilted by Elsie Vredenburg
73½" x 73½", 1994
Silk and 100% cotton fabrics, French wire ribbon, and wool batting are included in this quilt. Dimensional techniques including ruching, rolled flowers, layered flowers, folded flowers, and beading are used with hand appliqué and quilting.

121
CEILTEACH CIRCLES
Photo on page 7
CATHY GRAFTON
Pontiac, Illinois
74" x 74", 1997 to 1998
Quilt inspired by 18th century tablecloth embroidered with a wreath of flowers. Quilt's wreath made of silk ribbons, silk threads, and free-cut appliqué flowers. Divided border technique inspired by a Bayeaux Tapestry in France. Silk ribbon embroidery used as strong element in equal partnership with fabric appliqué, not just as embellishment.

122
BALTIMORE ANNUM
DIANE BURTON ROBB
Holland, Michigan
71" x 71", 1998
Center medallion represents Diane's house. Details in each quadrant reflect a different season of the year to correspond to surrounding calendar blocks. Appliquéd oak leaves are gradated for color according to seasons, beginning with spring's pale greens and ending with winter browns.

123
IN ABSENCE OF COLOR
CHARLEROI GROUP
Grindstone, Pennsylvania
quilted by Karen Phillips
60" x 60", 1997 to 1998
Quilt designed by Karen Phillips as group project to learn appliqué and embroidery techniques found in Baltimore album-style quilts. As group met to work on quilt, thoughts, questions, dilemmas, and general conversation were recorded and each step photographed. This documentation will remain with quilt and be auctioned off to benefit Children's Hospital of Pittsburgh.

124
A HAUNTED CASTLE IN BALTIMORE
Photo on page 22
LYNNE BOWBEER
Saline, Michigan
104" x 104", 1992 to 1998
Lynne had just finished a sampler quilt and thought it would be fun to use her favorite Castle Wall block as setting for her Baltimore blocks. Thus the concept of "haunted castle" and "ghost" of an album block in center and appliquéd ghosts on the backing. Hand appliquéd and quilted.

127
LOVE FLOWER
HISAKO ISOMURA
Osaka, Japan
158cm x 158cm, 1997 to 1998
Inspired by a Baltimore album quilt seen in the United States, Hisako went home to Japan to begin looking for suitable fabrics. She selected cottons and gradations of silk. She will give this quilt to her daughter as a sign of her life.

128
GO LOVELY ROSE
Photo on page 30
BALTIMORE ALBUM FRIENDS GROUP
Kingaroy, Queensland, Australia
58" x 58", 1994 to 1996
After a 1994 workshop on silk ribbon flowers, Elly offered Marjorie McKewen a challenge to make a quilt which included wreaths, hearts, and inscriptions. Quilt was made by nine friends who met monthly to accomplish this challenge.

129
JODY'S QUILT
GERRY SMITH
Cape Cod, Massachusetts
78" x 77", 1993 to 1996
Quilt submitted by deceased maker's daughter. For two of the three years Gerry worked on this quilt, she battled cancer. She died before she had time to complete all the quilting. Friends and acquaintances in her quilting guild took it upon themselves to complete it. This gesture of caring and remembrance and the quilt's core feeling of optimism is deeply rooted in Gerry's unflinching determination to live life fully despite illness.

Category #2

REVIVAL OF A CLASSIC STYLE

Sponsored by P&B Textiles

400
BALTIMORE—ONCE AGAIN
ARDETH J. LAAKE
Belmond, Iowa
82" x 82", 1994 to 1995
Sixteen-block quilt made from 100% cotton fabrics and batting, silks, and silk ribbon embellishment. Many blocks signed or inked by Ardeth with Pigma pen. Maryland Manor House resembles Ardeth's 100-year-old house, goose girl is symbolic of her grandmother's home. She likes to think it represents her grandmother coming for a visit.

401
BALTIMORE GARDEN ALBUM
DARLA JO HANKS
Forest City, Iowa
83" x 83", 1995 to 1997
Quilt was made for Darla's family and is intended to stay in the family. Consists of 100% cotton fabrics, wire-edged ribbon, rayon ribbon, silk ribbon, seed beads, embroidery floss, and Pigma pen. Block patterns come from various quilt artists and have lattice strips and a vine and ruched rose border.

402
BLEST BE THE TIES THAT BIND
Photo on page 23
CAPE COD CHAPTER OF THE GOOD LADIES OF BALTIMORE
Dennis, Massachusetts
70" x 82½", 1995 to 1998
Cape Cod Chapter of the Good Ladies of Baltimore was created to fulfill Elly's dream for someone to replicate album quilt #6 with white silk roses in the center from *Dimensional Appliqué*. The Abby Aldrich Rockefeller Center granted permission for replication and a transparency of the original quilt was received, enlarged, and photocopied. A trip was made to Williamsburg, Virginia and the quilt was examined square by square. Fabrics, colors, embroidery, appliqué, measurements, and quilting designs were documented. Reflecting on the past three years affirms the meaning of quilting to this group: friendships, talent, steadfastness, endurance, perseverance, and completion of a given task.

403
BALTIMORE ALBUM
DIXIE WRIGHT
Poulsbo, Washington
90" x 90", 1994 to 1997
Dixie feels that while all quilts have their own intrinsic merit, none seem so elegant as the well-executed Baltimore; few things speak to her so eloquently of more gracious times that fostered fine workmanship and open expressions of affection between family members and friends. This quilt is the triumph of optimism over experience. Perfecting appliqué skills along the way, the quilt was made primarily for the pleasure of stitching it and the satisfaction of owning a Baltimore she made herself.

Great peace is found in little busy-ness.
— Geoffrey Chaucer

404
BALTIMORE ALBUM BEAUTIE
Photo on page 29
PEARL BRAUN DYCK
Plum Coulee, Manitoba, Canada
90½" x 90½", 1993 to 1997
With inspiration from Anne Morrison and through monthly Saturday classes, the quilt was created. As the appliqué blocks became more intricate and time consuming, Pearl took them wherever she went, drawing interest from people who saw them. She considers it a gift to be able to work in this wonderful art of quiltmaking and looks forward to making many more quilts. One of these, most certainly, will be another Baltimore Album Quilt.

405
BALTIMORE COUNTRY
Photo on page 9
FRANCES ABELL BRAND
West Dennis, Massachusetts
68" x 68", 1996 to 1997
Frances's intention was to give her quilt an informal country look. Blocks were chosen accordingly. Hand quilted and appliquéd, quilt expresses enthusiasm and eagerness she felt about making a Baltimore Album quilt after receiving a gift of one of Elly's books from her husband. After collecting all the *Baltimore Beauties and Beyond* series books, she is grateful for Elly's masterful gift of encouragement and superb instruction in the appliqué technique that radiates from her books.

406
MATTHEW'S QUILT—BRIDGES FROM YESTERDAY TO TOMORROW
MARTHA EDENFIELD STOKES
Pensacola Beach, Florida
86" x 86", 1993 to 1996
Quilt was begun in a class taught by Dixie Haywood, and completed with Dixie's wonderful teaching methods, techniques, and unfailing encouragement over three and one-half years. Martha's passion for appliqué continues to grow and she never ceases to be amazed how much she has learned and the satisfaction that comes with quilting, but is constantly reminded of how far she has to go.

407
BALTIMORE ALBUM
Photo on page 24
DARLENE SCOW
Salt Lake City, Utah
84" x 84", 1997 to 1998
As appliqué quilts are Darlene's favorite, quilt was completed in about seven months. It contains several hearts (which appear in all of Darlene's quilts), both appliquéd and quilted. It is made from 100% cotton fabrics, poly-down batting, and a bit of gold floss for accent.

408
BALTIMORE BLOOMS IN 3-D
Photo on page 26
MARIAN K. BROCKSCHMIDT
Springfield, Illinois
72" x 72", 1995
Marian confessed she is "hooked on Baltimores." This is her fifth Baltimore, but she has already finished her sixth and is working on her seventh. Quilt features the Lord's Prayer in a central medallion and includes Rose of Sharon border with blanket stitch embroidery. There are dimensional flowers made from cotton, silk, ribbon and rick-rack.

409
BALTIMORE ROSE
Photo on page 27
SHARON FLUECKINGER
Rapid City, South Dakota
76½" x 99½", 1996 to 1997
Three fabrics were used to complete thirty-five paper-cut blocks for quilt—appliquéd, quilted, and bound—all by hand. This quilt will stay with Sharon and her husband for now. Her husband supports her interest in quilting, but not enough to cut and stitch. She appliqués on fishing and camping trips.

410
TO KELLY WITH LOVE
Photo on page 26
JUDI ROBB
Manhattan, Kansas
83" x 83", 1989 to 1994
Judi made this twenty-five block quilt because it was a challenge. She got together with friends once a month for a year to work on blocks, which contain folded flowers, stuffed work, ruched flowers, reverse appliqué, embroidery, couching, piecing, and handwritten family information. Hand quilted around each piece with a grid quilted in the background.

411
FAMILY ALBUM QUILT
Photo on page 19
MARGERY MCCARTHY
Taupo, New Zealand
80" x 92½", 1991 to 1996
Made for Margery's daughter, quilt is a memory album documenting family history from her great, great, great grandmother, who emigrated from Poland to Germany to New Zealand in 1876, to herself, including both maternal and paternal families. Included on the back is "future" block for Anna to fill in more details later.

412
BALTIMORE ALBUM TOMBSTONE
CATHY ORTEGA
Walnut, California
106" x 106", 1993 to 1997
Quilt was begun in a year-long class. Goal was to make one block each month. Many of the 150 students gave up, but Cathy was hooked. She continued machine piecing, hand appliquéing, hand quilting, inking, beading and silk ribbon embroidering. 'To sash or not to sash' torments her to this day. The dark red cut-work block needed an inscription in the center, so she made that block her tombstone with, "When you see this, Remember me." When she has gone, the blank will be filled in.

Play is the exultation of the possible.
— Martin Buber

413
SURPRISES
ANN ARBUCKLE
Anderson, California
81" x 81", 1993 to 1995
This is Ann's second Album Quilt and contains dimensional appliqué, reverse appliqué, *broderie perse*, silk roses, ruched roses and baskets, stuffed work, and pen work. Surprises appear at closer viewing. Ann would like to thank Elly for her wonderful books, which enable thousands of quilters to make memorable heirlooms for themselves and their families. Album Quilts satisfy the creative urge to do something old as new and inventive, and to help them understand the women that came before them and understand themselves better.

414
MOMMA'S GONNA BUY YOU A MOCKING BIRD
Photo on page 30
PATRICIA C. LUCEY
Boxford, Massachusetts
80" x 80", 1995 to 1998
Quilt was made in celebration of Patricia's family and their names are inscribed accordingly. It was started as a demonstration of 3-dimensional flower blocks for a Baltimore class and continued to grow because of the delight Patricia received in making each block. The quilt's name came from both the favorite lullaby of her children and the birds that bring great joy in sight and sound to her world.

415
MADE IN CALIFORNIA
Photo on page 22
NANCY BUSBY
Rio Vista, California
92" x 92", 1990 to 1994
Print and solid 100% cotton fabrics were used for this sixteen-block quilt. It has hand appliqué, script lettering, embellishment, and hand-quilting techniques. Four of the blocks are Nancy's original designs. Each block signed and dated as it was finished to help document the time involved in making such a quilt.

416
BALTIMORE REVISITED
DONNA M. KERR
Bradenton, Florida
90" x 90", 1992 to 1998
Donna has always loved appliqué and admired the Baltimore style with all the beautiful bouquets of flowers and birds. Quilt was made as family heirloom and contains 100% cotton fabrics, French ribbon, rayon ribbon, China silk, rayon seam binding, synthetic fabric, and inkings. It depicts her love of her country and to show how proud she is to be an American. Bible verses and sayings inked on some blocks show her love and belief in her God.

417
UNTITLED
KATHRYN BYRNE
Trabuco Canyon, California
83" x 83", 1994 to 1997
Kathryn began quilt to help her forget
how unhappy she was after a traumatic
move her family made. She wanted to
begin a major quilt project and after
seeing Elly's work, a Baltimore Album
quilt for her husband seemed like the
right project to embark on. Hand
appliquéd, quilted, and embellished.

418
BALTIMORE ALBUM
ALICE M. BACHRATY
Williamsville, New York
78" x 78", 1989 to 1991
A friend gave Alice a stack of about
twenty pieces of a red print fabric that
were "cut-offs" from a dress factory. This
finally pushed Alice into actually starting
quilt after twenty years of thinking about
it. This fabric became signature fabric in
quilt and a tribute to their friendship.

419
LOVE IS THE MUSIC
ZOLALEE GAYLOR
Midwest City, Oklahoma
96" x 96", 1991 to 1998
Quilt consists of blocks made as class
samples for a year-long class she taught.
Her first love is her church and her
second is music. Coming in a close third
is needlework. The blocks help combine
all three loves in a tribute to the ladies
of Baltimore for their legacy of beautiful
presentation quilts.

420
ALBUM OF FRIENDSHIP
Photo on page 15
DEBRA BALLARD
Midland, Michigan
quilted by Elsie Vredenburg
81½" x 81½", 1990 to 1992
Blocks were made as teaching samples
for album class taught by Debra. She has
been very fortunate to have made several
close friends during this class (they continue to meet), so she named quilt
Album of Friendship in honor of
these friends.

421
QUILT FOR ELOISE
Photo on page 13
JUDY BONNER
North Richmond, NSW, Australia
83" x 83", 1996 to 1998
Judy's first attempt at dimensional and
hand appliqué, inking and hand quilting.
Quilt named for daughter who inspired
maker to create such a special quilt. Judy
knows one day her family will appreciate
the quilt and she hopes they will love it
and feel the love that has gone into it.

What we play is life.
— Louis Armstrong

423
BALTIMORE BRIDE QUILT
CHRIS KINKA
Sturgeon Bay, Wisconsin
80" x 80", 1990 to 1997
Chris hopes her quilt will speak to those
who see it, just as those quilts of long
ago spoke to her. She would like it to be
a reminder of the ladies of Baltimore—
then and now. Quilt is a family heirloom
and will leave a lasting impression and
impart the true love of the Baltimores,
as she experienced it.

424
BARBARA'S BALTIMORE
BARBARA COLLINS
Arroyo Grande, California
74" x 90", 1991 to 1994
Barbara's Swiss heritage influenced the
use of color, especially bright tones. She
looked in the garden for "correctness" in
what colors should be together. What a
freedom that observation gave her as she
realized that everything goes together in
nature. She particularly enjoyed hunting
for just the right fabrics.

425
SUNSHINE DOES BALTIMORE
SUNSHINE QUILTERS OF SAN DIEGO,
APPLI-QUILTERS
San Diego, California
82" x 97", 1996 to 1998
After learning new Baltimore appliqué
techniques monthly for over two years,
the Appli-quilters decided to create a
Baltimore album quilt as their guild's
opportunity quilt. Kits and patterns
were handed out at the October, 1996
Sunshine Quilters of San Diego guild
meeting to those who wanted to make
a block. The blocks were returned in
March, 1997. The Appli-quilters then
chose the border battern, and each took
one side home to work on. The quilt
was then layered and quilted.

426
FLOWERS FOR LEAH
DIANE EARDLEY
Santa Barbara, California
60" x 60", 1996 to 1998
Diane looks at her grandmother's
exquisite Rose of Sharon quilt and feels
her presence. The most valuable posses-
sions she has from her ancestors are her
grandmother's quilts, so she created this
quilt in the hopes that her grandchildren
will look at this quilt and feel her
presence.

427
RIBBONS AND ROSES
SUSAN KURTH
Oklahoma City, Oklahoma
99" x 101", 1990 to 1992
Recovering from kidney transplant
surgery, Susan decided to try her hand
at appliqué and began this quilt. The
ruched flowers and stuffed roses are
"all some sleezy acetate that raveled like
crazy," but at the time she was trying to
learn to appliqué, the frayed edges
seemed the least of her problems. Quilt
was completed, but she wished she had
more appliqué experience before starting.

428

BALTIMORE BLOOMS II
Photo on page 29
ANN HOLDEN PLUMMER
Pleasanton, California
90" x 90", 1995 to 1998
Ann enjoyed mixing inking, embroidery, ruching, silhouetting, bead work, cutaway appliqué, and hand quilting techniques in quilt. She hopes quilt speaks to her descendants and tells them something about her and life in late 20th century. She has never considered herself an artist, but knows these quilts call to her, and she gets a great deal of satisfaction from Baltimore album-style quilts.

*What is all this juice
and all this joy?*
— Gerard Manley Hopkins

429

*BALTIMORE COMES TO
THE PRAIRIE*
Photo on page 11
PRAIRIE QUILT GUILD
Wichita, Kansas
93" x 108", 1998
Quilt became a reality because of work of twenty-nine talented quilters who created blocks, appliquéd swags, assembled and quilted this wonderfully traditional red and green Baltimore album-style quilt. Many of these women would never attempt an entire Baltimore album quilt, but one block was possible. They each accepted their assignment with relish.

430

KINDAMO FAMILY ALBUM
Photo on page 19
CORINE BUECHNER
Marcell, Minnesota
quilted by Mona Cumberledge
90" x 90", 1996 to 1997
Quilt made to commemorate ten wonderful years of marriage. Making this quilt helped to slow down the pace of Corine's life. It allowed her to experience the peace and joy of every moment she has the good fortune to spend quilting.

431

*THESE ARE A FEW OF
MY FAVORITE THINGS*
SUSAN VANDERVEEN
El Cajon, California
80" x 95", 1994 to 1998
Quilt is a tribute to Susan's pets, past and present, as well as the her favorite things: flowers, meadowlarks, butterflies, color, and quilting. It contains wired ribbon roses and buds, 3-dimensional flowers, silk floss, ribbon embroidery, and quilting.

Category #3

**REFLECTIVE OF A PARTICULAR LIFE
AND TIME**

Sponsored by Fiskars, Inc.

700

*THE FRIENDSHIP, LOVE, AND
TRUTH QUILT*
Photo on page 14
KATHRYN F. TENNYSON
Chestertown, New York
80" x 92", 1991 to 1994

Quilt made as a memorial to Kathryn's mother Kathryn Little Flachbarth. She hopes quilt's life has just begun and that her children, grandchildren and their descendants will remember her and her mother through this quilt. She feels her mother would have been very proud to know of her efforts and achievements reflected in this quilt. It truly shows her deep and abiding love for her mother.

701

ELLY MIX
HELEN HAUN
Fort Bragg, California
74" x 74", 1996 to 1998
Helen, born in her grandmother's sewing room, has made needle and thread a very big part of her life. She was sent away by her grandmother to teach her to change from left-handed to right-handed, but after a time the school phoned and said "Come and get this girl, she's not going to change." She loves to create beauty wherever she can.

702

FAMILY "PHOTO" ALBUM
MARILYN ROBINSON
St. Peters, Missouri
79" x 80", 1994
Each month a quilt group of seven chose a design to stitch and put in a quarter-yard of fabric. At the end of the month those who finished their block would be in a drawing to win the fabric. Marilyn's quilt is truly a family treasure and special to her because of the many personal touches and the insight she gained into the group creative effort that must have been a part of those Baltimore album quilts of long ago and their makers.

703

BACK ROAD TO BALTIMORE
JULIE ISELIN TURJOMAN
Upper Montclair, New Jersey
69" x 69", 1993 to 1997
Quilt is named *Back Road to Baltimore* because Julie definitely did not travel the super-highway with this project. Her meandering permitted her to explore and utilize a somewhat non-traditional color scheme. Quilt is reflective of a time in her life; divorce, reflection and renewal, and a joyful new beginning in a wonderful new marriage.

*Painting is just another
way of keeping a diary.*
— Pablo Picasso

704

CARMEL BY THE SEA ALBUM
Photo on page 21
JEANNIE OLIVERIA
Pacific Grove, California
75" x 90", 1996 to 1998
Jeannie believes the variety in fashioning Baltimore album quilts meets her deepest craving for creativity and the album process offers the opportunity to explore a wide variety of needlework skills. She is drawn to album quilts by their unrivaled beauty and historical significance.

705

LITTLE BROWN BIRD

Photo on page 28

MARGARET DOCHERTY

Durham, United Kingdon

84" x 84½", 1994 to 1997

Quilt made for Margaret's daughter Mary who wondered aloud why her mother couldn't make a "pretty quilt." This shocked the maker, coming from a daughter heavily into "grunge," but the challenge was accepted. Design inspiration came from many places: traditional Baltimore quilts, modern blocks, Margaret's own country garden, and quiltmakers of the past.

707

IN LOVING MEMORY

CHRISTINE HANSEN KMAK

Leesburg, Virginia

63" x 63", 1997 to 1998

Quilt made in memory of Christine's mother (Lucile Amelia Kelsey Hansen) who passed away when maker was eight years old. The use of solely black-and-white fabrics in quilt is reflective of the only photos she has of her mother. Quilt contains French satins, velvets, taffetas, and wired velvet and organdy ribbons.

708

SUSAN'S SERENITY

Photo on page 27

SUSAN E. HINZMAN

Bethesda, Maryland

91" x 91", 1993 to 1996

Susan keeps an idea journal of jokes, jottings, clippings, notes, pictures, thoughts . . . anything that tickles her funny bone or strikes her creative eye. Many of the ideas that appear on quilt can be found in the journal—including foxes (fifty-five of them), a lighthouse, bunnies, ponies, geese, and flowers.

709

CANADA ALBUM

DIANNE DOUGLAS

Saskatoon, Canada

76" x 76", 1998

Quilt consists of different sized blocks and was intended to reflect love and pride Dianne feels for her country, and to answer the question posed by a friend newly arrived in Canada, "What does it mean to be a Canadian?"

710

GRANDMOTHER'S CLOSET

RONDA MCALLEN

Pearland, Texas

70" x 70", 1998

Quilt is tribute to Ronda's grandmother's closet. It served as a reading refuge whenever the chatter of cousins and family were overwhelming and its light was comforting during summer thunderstorms. Ronda remembers sewing with her grandmother and the smell of coffee and vanilla from the divinity candy she always made still lingering in the air.

711

SEASONS OF THE GRANGE

TRUDY FREY

Phillipsburg, New Jersey

86½" x 86½", 1996

Quilt depicts symbols of the Grange, which was organized to improve lives of farm families and fight the railroad's monopoly. The Grange is a secret fraternal organization that gave equal rights to women. Today, the Grange is concerned about families and rapidly changing rural environment and works to enrich its members and their community. Ritual and symbols remain as they were at the Grange's conception.

712

BRIDGING THE PAST AND THE FUTURE

NANCY LOUISE WELLS

Guelph, Ontario, Canada

73" x 73", 1997 to 1998

Quilt images chosen reflect childhood memories of Nancy's grandmother's garden and her love of all types of flowers, wildflowers, and grapevines growing in and around her family cottage; the beautiful peacocks seen on visits to the zoo; and her own love of flowers and gardening.

713

THE LADY'S RED HAT

Photo on page 16

PHYLLIS A. STREET

Honaker, Virginia

82" x 82", 1994 to 1996

Quilt was the release of grief from her husband's illness and death from cancer and her own recovery from a first round of cancer. With lots of fun, laughter, and good-natured input from Phyllis's family and quilting friends, quilt was made to celebrate the return of color and joy to her life.

714

TAMIKI MAKAU RAU

JEAN K. NUTTER

Auckland, New Zealand

101" x 102", 1996 to 1998

In Maori, the quilt's name means "desired by hundreds." Quilt is a montage of Auckland: including a house, native flowers, birds, a sailboat, a meeting house, a fisherman—all things that have meaning to Jean and her country.

715

MY BALTIMORE BEAUTY

MARY ALICE SOVRAN

Raleigh, North Carolina

89" x 89", 1991 to 1998

Quilt was intended to portray family history and was begun by taking a class that met once a month for a year. Work continued as Mary Alice moved from Arizona to North Carolina. She continues to learn about Baltimore album quilts, teach classes, and stitch more blocks.

716

THIS IS MY STORY, THIS IS MY SONG
MARTHA W. GINN
Hattiesburg, Mississippi
84" x 100", 1990 to 1995
Quilt contains blocks that commemorate important events in Martha's life, among which is her favorite verse from her religious heritage—"And what doth the Lord require of thee, but to do justly, and to love mercy, and to walk humbly with thy God?" Micah 6:8. Also included are blocks designed for members of her family.

Every blade of grass has its Angel that bends over it and whispers, "Grow, grow."
— The Talmud

717

BLESS THEM, O GOD!
SUSAN KURTH
Oklahoma City, Oklahoma
88½" x 88½", 1995 to 1998
Quilt was made to honor the volunteers who gave their time in the search and care for the victims following the bombing of the Alfred P. Murrah Federal Building. Commemorative quilts are made in the effort to make something beautiful following a time of struggle, violence, or tragedy.

718

PAPERCUTS & PATCHWORK
SUZANNE PEERY SCHUTT
Clinton, Mississisippi
76½" 95½", 1996 to 1998
Suzanne overdyed some of the fabrics to emulate the vegetable dyes used in mid-19th century prints. Quilt dedicated to maker's father-in-law who had a smile that embraced everyone.

719

BA'WAS
BEA MULLINS
Dayton, Ohio
62" x 62", 1997 to 1998
Quilt was made as a personal challenge and as a tribute to uplifting friendship. Bea chose to interpret the Baltimore blocks as black-and-white photos which are shades and tints of gray with small amounts of red and green. Native American culture has many legends that point to the butterflies as messengers to heaven; thus the quilt was named for the Caddo Indian Tribe's word for butterfly.

720

FAMILY QUILT
SUE SMITH
Stilwell, Kansas
71" x 84", 1997 to 1998
Inspiration began with the Family Pets block and developed; includes names of pets over forty years and the inscription "Love in the middle with Charity, Honesty, Gratitude, Faith & Fairness." The plan is to share quilt with each family for one year. Exchange is to take place at Christmastime when everyone is together.

721

MEMORIES OF LIFE'S DIFFERENT PATHS
ROSEMARY YOUNGS
Walker, Michigan
83½" x 83½", 1996 to 1998
After finding out she had multiple sclerosis, Rosemary felt if she could do one more quilt by hand, it would be a Baltimore album. Sunbonnet Sues and Overall Bills represent family members. Hand quilting became difficult, but she didn't give up. Finally the binding and labels were added and it was completed. Her quilting will now take a different path: to machine quilting, but this will not be her last quilt.

722

AMAZING GRACE
JEANNIE COLLINS-ARDERN
Oakville, Ontario, Canada
93" x 93", 1994 to 1998
Quilt was created in Jeannie's personal quiet time, sitting in her garden or listening to classical music, occasionally with her husband, always with her dog. It became intricately linked with personal meditation and reflection, and over time, she began to associate quilt with a new-found sense of peace and acceptance of who and what she is.

723

BALTIMORE REVISITED
SHEILAH CLEARY
Monarch Beach, California
88" x 88", 1989 to 1994
Many quilters have found joy and solace in reestablishing the tradition of the Baltimore album. The opportunity for such personal involvement in a work of lasting beauty is much like giving birth and raising a child in the sense of immortality it provides. Sheilah felt at one with a woman of a long time ago who stitched by candlelight as she listened to the sounds of the harbor.

Every child is an artist. The problem is how to remain an artist once he grows up.
— Pablo Picasso

724

50TH ANNIVERSARY BALTIMORE
MARIAN K. BROCKSCHMIDT
Springfield, Illinois
68" x 68", 1992 to 1993
In 1992 Marian's husband was diagnosed with Non-Hodgkin's Lymphoma. As she began making their anniversary quilt in 1992, she kept praying the Lord would permit them to celebrate their 50th anniversary in 1993. Their prayers were answered, and they have since celebrated their 55th anniversary in 1998.

About the Author

*E*lly Sienkiewicz has written ten important needlework books for C&T Publishing. Nine of these books comprise the Baltimore Beauties® series, begun in 1989. Elly places a complex historical style—the Baltimore-style Album Quilts—within the grasp of every late 20th century quiltmaker through her clear instruction and authentic patterns. Her leadership sustains this revival, now fifteen years strong. In a linked fellowship, those who love this style have taken it to something clearly "Beyond Baltimore".

Elly's path from career woman to stay-at-home mom of three, led her to become an early professional in the nascent quilt movement of the early '70s. Elly notes that her Wellesley College Class of 1964 is a "cusp generation"—women who as freshmen expected to live their mothers' 1950s societal ideal, but who were the object of radically different expectations by the time they graduated. Elly herself earned a Masters of Science degree and taught high school for seven years. A history major with a lifetime love of needleart, Elly's traditionalist desire to stay home once her children arrived led to home-centered enterprises related to the burgeoning quilt world industry. Her experiences range from quilting teacher, to retail mail-order proprietess, to respected quiltmaker, to author, historian, and president of the Elly Sienkiewicz Appliqué Academy. Elly's devotion as a teacher, her concern for her students, and her love for quiltmaking have made her a cherished mentor. Elly lives in Washington, DC with her husband Stan and, whenever they can be there too, their children Alex, Katya, and Donald and wife Katja.

The meaning of Life is to see.
— Hui Neng

OTHER BOOKS BY ELLY SIENKIEWICZ

Appliqué Paper Greetings!

Romancing Ribbons into Flowers

Papercuts and Plenty, Volume III

Baltimore Album Revival!

Appliqué 12 Borders and Medallions!

Dimensional Appliqué

Design a Baltimore Album Quilt

Appliqué 12 Easy Ways!

Baltimore Beauties and Beyond, Volume II

Baltimore Album Quilts

Baltimore Beauties and Beyond, Volume I

Spoken Without A Word

OTHER FINE BOOKS BY C&T PUBLISHING

The Art of Silk Ribbon Embroidery, Judith Baker Montano

The Artful Ribbon, Candace Kling

Crazy Quilt Handbook, Judith Montano

Crazy Quilt Odyssey, Judith Montano

Deidre Scherer, Work in Fabric and Thread, Deidre Scherer

Elegant Stitches, An Illustrated Stitch Guide & Source Book of Inspiration, Judith Baker Montano

Enduring Grace, Quilts from the Shelburne Museum Collection, Celia Y. Oliver

Focus on Features, Life-like Portrayals in Appliqué, Charlotte Warr Anderson

Forever Yours, Wedding Quilts, Clothing & Keepsakes, Amy Barickman

Free Stuff for Quilters on the Internet, Judy Heim and Gloria Hansen

Hand Quilting with Alex Anderson, Six Projects for Hand Quilters

Heirloom Machine Quilting, Third Edition, Harriet Hargrave

Imagery on Fabric, Second Edition, Jean Ray Laury

Jacobean Rhapsodies, Composing with 28 Appliqué Designs, Patricia B. Campbell and Mimi Ayars

Judith B. Montano, Art & Inspirations, Judith B. Montano

Mariner's Compass Quilts, New Directions, Judy Mathieson

Mastering Machine Appliqué, Harriet Hargrave

Quilts from the Civil War, Nine Projects, Historical Notes, Diary Entries, Barbara Brackman

Trapunto by Machine, Hari Walner

Wildflowers, Designs for Appliqué and Quilting, Carol Armstrong

SOURCE

The Cotton Patch Mail Order
3405 Hall Lane, Dept. CTB
Layayette, CA 94549
e-mail: cottonpa@aol.com
800-835-4418
925-283-7883
A Complete Quilting Supply Store

FOR MORE INFORMATION WRITE FOR A FREE CATALOG

C&T Publishing, Inc.
P.O. Box 1456
Lafayette, CA 94549
(800) 284-1114
http://www.ctpub.com
email: ctinfo@ctpub.com